I CHOOSE
Empathy

I CHOOSE SERIES

ELIZABETH ESTRADA

Copyright 2021 by Elizabeth Estrada - All rights reserved.
Published and printed in the USA.

No part of this publication or the information in it may be quoted or
reproduced in any form by means of printing, scanning, photocopying,
or otherwise without permission of the copyright holder.

I CHOOSE
Empathy

ELIZABETH ESTRADA

Have you ever seen someone unhappy, looking a little sad.
And even though you don't know what's going on, you feel bad?
Have you ever seen someone crying and wanted to cry too?
Listening and comforting them was all that you could do.

Well, this feeling of wanting to help has a special name.
And once you have it in you, you will never be the same.
It's called empathy which means you care how others feel,
Having compassion and showing kindness is more than ideal.

Being able to feel empathy and care deeply for those you know
Is a pure sign of humanity and it helps us to grow.
Having empathy is not only for sadness or when people are feeling blue.
It can also be for happiness or excitement, too.

You can be empathetic and feel happy for others' joy,
You can feel positive on a friend's birthday when they get a brand new toy,
Or when they win a carnival game after playing hard and trying.
No, empathy doesn't only set in when another person is crying.

When someone's feeling angry and steaming, full of rage,
If you have empathy, you'll feel as if you're on the same page.
They may yell and be in an angry zone.
But when you listen, they won't feel so alone.

Some say having empathy is a very special gift.
It's like during a rain shower and you see that rainbows do exist.
Empathy means we are kind to others and understand.
When people receive empathy, they are more willing to lend a hand.

I say having empathy can also be a choice.
You can choose to be empathetic by using your voice.
Tell others you understand them when they're feeling a certain way,
And be compassionate and caring every single day.

Be authentic and kind in everything you do.
Give to others as much as you would hope they would give to you.
When you see someone having a tough time, don't put more on their backs.
If someone else is hungry, share with them your snacks!

When someone's feeling happy, celebrate with them if you can.
Or when someone's feeling scared, go ahead and reach out your hand.
Being empathetic is saying and showing that you care.
If that person needs you, you'll always be right there.

So, the next time you find yourself with
Someone whose feelings are on display,
Sit next to them, pat their back, and tell them
It's going to be okay.

And you know what? They probably
Will do this for someone else too.
Empathy is contagious — I've seen it
Spread, through and through!

Soon everywhere you look, people will
Be treating others in a positive way,
And together we'll be there for one
Another every single day.

Choose empathy when you can, and keep it in your mind.
For an empathetic person is truly a wonderful kind!

Printed in Great Britain
by Amazon